THE WEATHER REPORT

NORTHERN LIGHTS SIGHTING!

EDITED BY JOANNE RANDOLPH

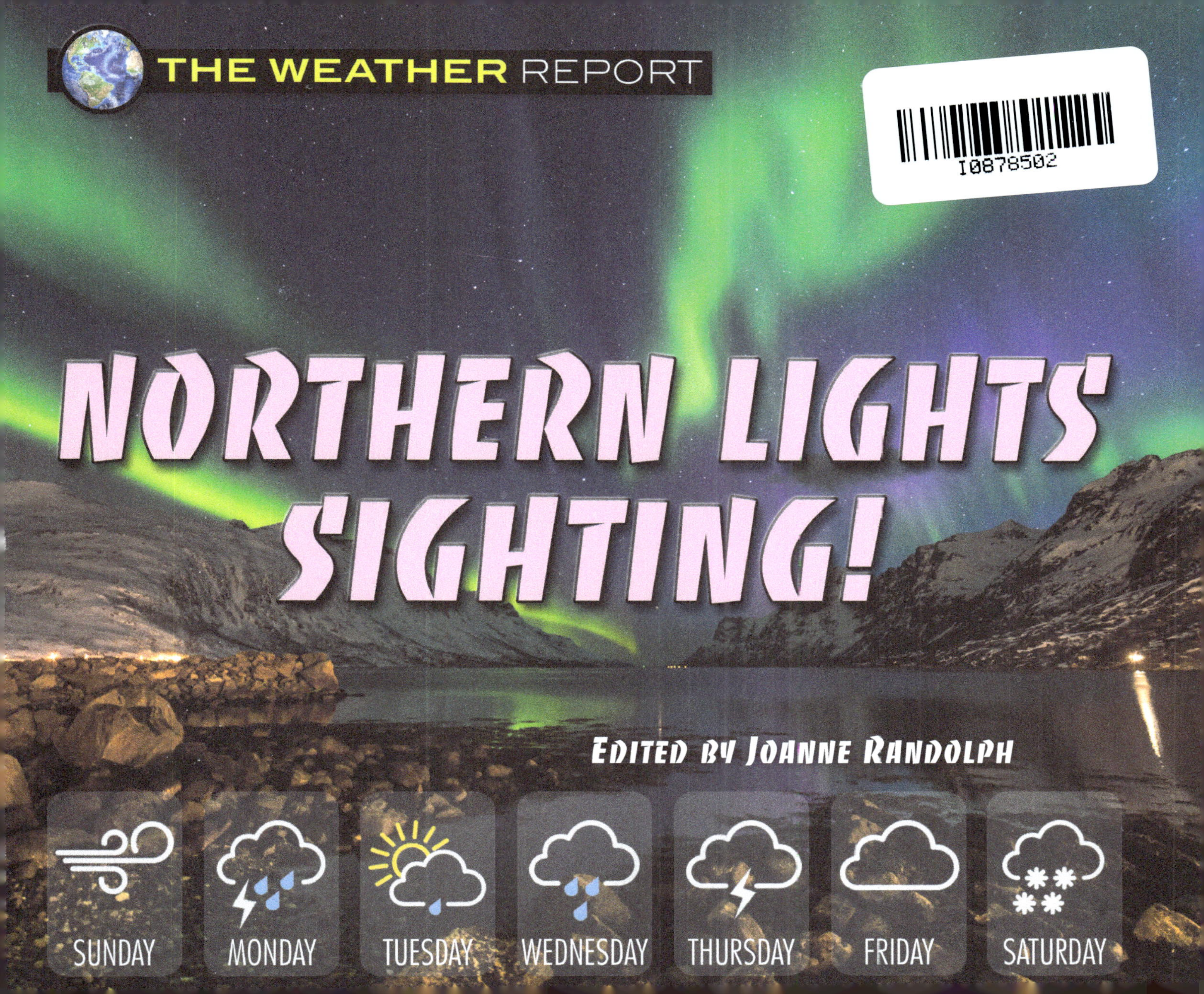

This edition published in 2018 by:
Enslow Publishing, LLC.
101 W. 23rd Street, Suite 240
New York, NY 10011

Cataloging-in-Publication Data

Names: Randolph, Joanne, editor.
Title: Northern lights sighting! / edited by Joanne Randolph.
Description: New York : Enslow Publishing, 2018 | Series: The weather report |
Includes bibliographical references and index. | Audience: Grades 3-5.
Identifiers: ISBN 9780766090231 (library bound) | ISBN 9780766090217 (pbk.) | ISBN 9780766090224 (6 pack)
Subjects: LCSH: Auroras--Juvenile literature.
Classification: LCC QC971.4 N67 2018 | DDC 538/.768--dc23Printed in the United States of America

To Our Readers: We have done our best to make sure all website addresses in this book were active and appropriate when we went to press. However, the author and the publisher have no control over and assume no liability for the material available on those websites or on any websites they may link to. Any comments or suggestions can be sent by e-mail to customerservice@enslow.com.

Photos credits: Cover, p. 1 V. Belov/Shutterstock.com (northern lights), solarseven/Shutterstock.com (weather symbols); series logo, NPeter/Shutterstock.com; interior pages background image, back cover, Sabphoto/Shutterstock.com; pp. 3, 28, 30, 32 Igor Zh./Shutterstock.com; pp. 4, 8, 17, 23 US Air Force photo by Senior Airman Joshua Strang; p. 5 ZinaidaSopina/Shutterstock.com; p. 6 Doug McLean/Shutterstock.com; p. 9 AFP/Getty Images; p. 11 Science Source; p. 13 Roger Harris/Science Photo Library/Getty Images; p. 14 Time Life Pictures/The LIFE Picture Collection/Getty Images; p. 15 NASA; p. 18 NASA/Getty Images; p. 19 NASA/Corbis/Getty Images; p. 20 NASA/Science Photo Library/Getty Images; p. 21 Mark Garlick/Science Source; p. 25 Milagli/Shutterstock.com; p. 26 Danita Delimont/Gallo Images/Getty Images.

Article Credits: Alan Dyer, "When the Heavens Dance," *Odyssey*; Fiona Bayrock, "Auroras: To See or Not to See. . . Is the Question," *Odyssey*.

Contents

CHAPTER ONE

WHEN THE HEAVENS DANCE

How does nature stage a breathtaking light show called the aurora borealis? The night starts out like any other clear evening for stargazing . . . until an unusual green "cloud" appears across the northern sky. The cloud brightens and begins to take shape, forming rippling curtains. They grow in size and climb the sky, and then patches of red appear, as if the heavens are catching fire. It's like nothing you've ever seen before.

Then the sky explodes. The curtains shoot up and cover the sky, meeting straight above you, like searchlights or lasers playing across the heavens. But this display is much more complex and unpredictable. It's as if you're looking down a tunnel of shimmering light. All around you the colorful curtains ripple and dance, like luminous veils being blown in a wind high above your head. Bright greens mix with deep reds and pinks. You might even catch sight of subtle blue and purple tints as you

This photo of the aurora borealis was taken in Norway.

stand beneath the climax of nature's most spectacular light show. After a few minutes, the display dims and fades into random patches of light, switching off and on across the sky for the rest of the night.

What you have just witnessed is a grand display of northern lights, also known as the aurora borealis, the Latin words for "northern dawn."

Compare this photo of the aurora borealis to the previous one. It looks very different, doesn't it? In this one, it looks like streaks of red and green light in the sky.

Most people in North America might be lucky to see such an awe-inspiring spectacle once or twice a decade. Perhaps only once in a lifetime! People living in the northern United States (especially Alaska) and in Canada are more fortunate. They can see outstanding displays of northern lights every few months, with lesser displays shining in northern skies almost every week.

CHAPTER TWO

SOLAR EXPLOSIONS

Though displays of auroras have been recorded by cultures around the world for thousands of years, only in the last few decades have we begun to understand what causes the light shows. While the lights do happen in our **atmosphere**, for their ultimate cause we need to look all the way back to the sun.

Massive explosions near the surface of the sun called **flares** release more energy in seconds than humans have generated in all of history. What triggers these flares is still unclear. The sun's bright surface is a tangled carpet of **magnetic fields**, twisting and coiling. The magnetic fields reach up into the atmosphere of the sun, called the **corona**, a region of thin but superhot gas glowing at temperatures of millions of degrees. (Technically, matter so hot isn't called a gas, but a **plasma**—a state of matter made of **atoms** ripped apart into bare **nuclei** and free-flying **electrons**.)

The sun's complex magnetic fields can twist together like rubber bands, which then trap the superheated coronal gas. The fields store up energy until, like a rubber band that can't be twisted and stretched anymore, the fields snap. They suddenly release streams of intensely hot gas and searing **radiation** such as X-rays and **ultraviolet** light.

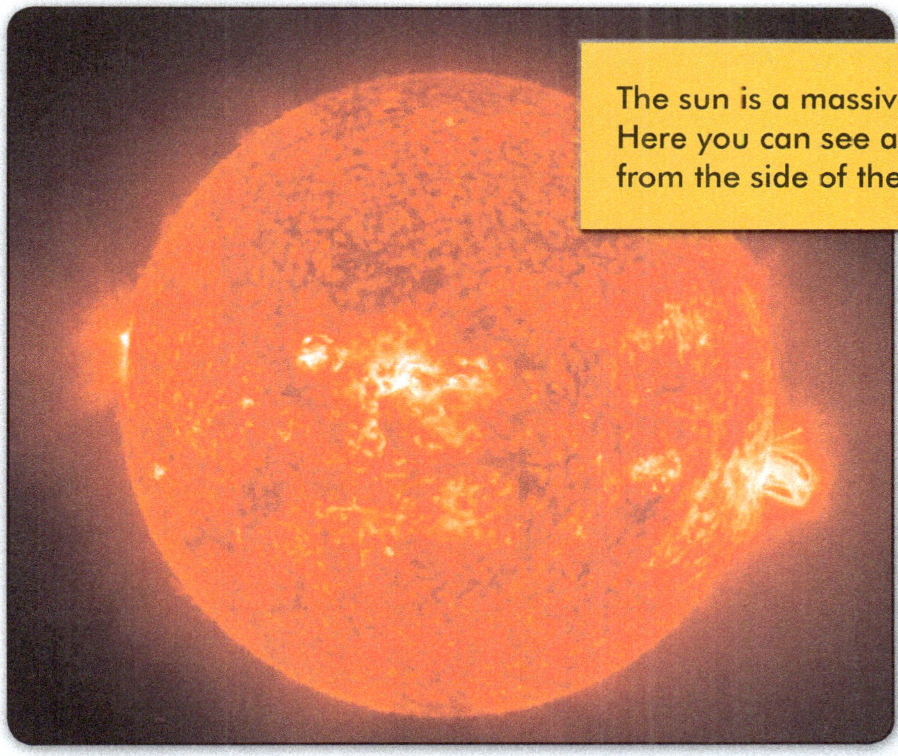

The sun is a massively hot star. Here you can see a flare exploding from the side of the sun.

Space Weather

The expanding gas and radiation can blow a bubble in the sun's weak atmosphere. The bubble bursts, blowing a cloud of **atomic particles** away from the sun and into space. This event is called a coronal mass ejection. In **time-lapse** movies from satellites such as the Solar and Heliospheric Observatory (SOHO), the mass ejections make the sun look as if it is blowing off puffs of smoke.

One of the earliest discoveries in the space age was that the space between the planets is always filled with atomic particles blowing from the sun, in what we call the solar wind. Like the wind you feel outside on a pleasant day, the wind from the sun usually blows in a gentle "breeze."

But those powerful solar flares can stir up storms in the solar wind. The bursting bubbles of the sun's atmosphere can shoot dense streams of particles at high speed across the solar system, creating the space version of a **squall** or windstorm on Earth. Sometimes, Earth lies directly in the path of one of these solar storms. About two or three days after it leaves the sun, the storm front reaches Earth and hits us with a **gale-force** blast of energized particles—electrons and **protons**—that were generated 93 million miles (149 million kilometers) away on the sun.

This image shows a coronal mass ejection (CME). From this angle, the sun is on top and the CME is beneath the sun. That is a huge amount of energy and matter being shot into space!

Magnetic Attraction

Fortunately, Earth has a "deflector shield" that usually protects us from the full blast of the solar storm cloud. The shield is our planet's magnetic field. Earth's molten interior generates a magnetic field that surrounds our planet and extends far into space. When solar wind particles reach Earth, they usually flow around our magnetic "force field," like water flowing around an island in a stream. But thousands of miles downstream, on the night side of Earth in our magnetic "tail," some of those streaming particles tunnel their way into our magnetic shield.

What happens then is still poorly understood, although orbiting satellites are beginning to provide a better picture. During an intense solar storm, our magnetic shield fills to the brim with energized particles that entered through the back door. These particles build up in number and intensity, like a battery being charged up. Then—zap! In a process perhaps similar to the twisting magnetic lines on the sun that created the storm in the first place, the magnetic-field lines downstream from our planet twist and pinch off. They squeeze the energetic particles and squirt them toward Earth at the breakneck speed of 932 miles (1,500 km) per second. The high-speed electrons and protons rain down onto our upper atmosphere from the region of space far above the night side of our planet.

This diagram shows Earth's magnetic fields, which extend from its magnetic poles (not its geographic poles).

Satellites orbit Earth and do many jobs, such as gathering data, providing cellular service, or taking pictures. The SOHO spends all its time collecting data from and taking pictures of the sun.

All Charged Up

The particles act like a beam of electricity (in fact, that's what they are) shooting through a **neon** lamp. The lamp is almost a **vacuum** inside, with just a small amount of neon gas. When charged up by a jolt of electric current, the atoms first absorb the shot of energy and then release it again in the form of light. The gas begins to glow.

In a similar process, the incoming beams of electrons and protons charge up atoms and molecules in our atmosphere such as oxygen and nitrogen. Zapped by the current of particles from space, these gases glow in shades of green, red, blue, and pink. Our atmosphere acts like a giant neon lamp being hit with a billion kilowatts of energy in just a few minutes.

All that energy pulses far above us. The curtains of northern lights start about 311 miles (500 km) up, so high that the space shuttle and space

This view of the aurora borealis from outer space was captured by the International Space Station in 2015.

station sometimes fly through the tops of aurora displays. Very intense displays can penetrate down to an altitude of 50 miles (80 km). Usually the brightest auroral light we see comes from heights of 62 to 75 miles (100 to 120 km). That's still ten times higher than most jet airliners fly and well within the layer of our atmosphere called the **ionosphere**, where the air is so thin that it remains a near vacuum. You couldn't breathe up where the aurora dances, but electricity can work its magic to create a colorful light show.

So, if you are lucky enough to see a display of northern lights, think about where the action started, 93 million miles (149 million km) away at the sun. You are seeing the power of electricity, magnetism, **chemistry**, and atomic **physics** working together to make the heavens dance.

CHAPTER THREE

CYCLES OF THE SUN

The sun has its ups and downs. Every eleven years the sun peaks in activity and erupts with more flares and coronal mass ejections. Dark regions of cool gas called sunspots break out over the surface. More auroras dance in our sky. This period of stormy solar behavior is called solar maximum and lasts one or two years.

Then, over several years, the sun quiets down. Only the occasional flare explodes, and the sun's face can go unblemished by sunspots for days at a time. Few auroras appear, especially at southern locations.

The dark spots on this image of the sun are sunspots. When there are more sunspots on the surface we have more auroras.

A solar maximum peaked in 2000, but some giant solar storms blew our way in 2001 and 2002, creating lifetime-best displays of northern lights in the spring and autumn of both years. The year 2016 marked the end of another solar maximum period. The next "solar max" is expected in 2019 or 2020. However, large flares can still erupt without warning, giving us nights of dancing auroras at any time.

This intense aurora happened on March 6, 2012, after one of the largest solar flares of the current solar cycle.

CIRCLES IN THE SKY

When electrons and protons beam down from the magnetic fields around our planet, they form a unique pattern in the sky. Seen from space, our atmosphere lights up in two glowing rings, each about 2,485 miles (4,000 km) wide. One ring is centered on the north magnetic pole in the Canadian Arctic, while the other is centered on the south magnetic pole in Antarctica. These rings are called auroral ovals—a bit misleading, as the rings are usually round.

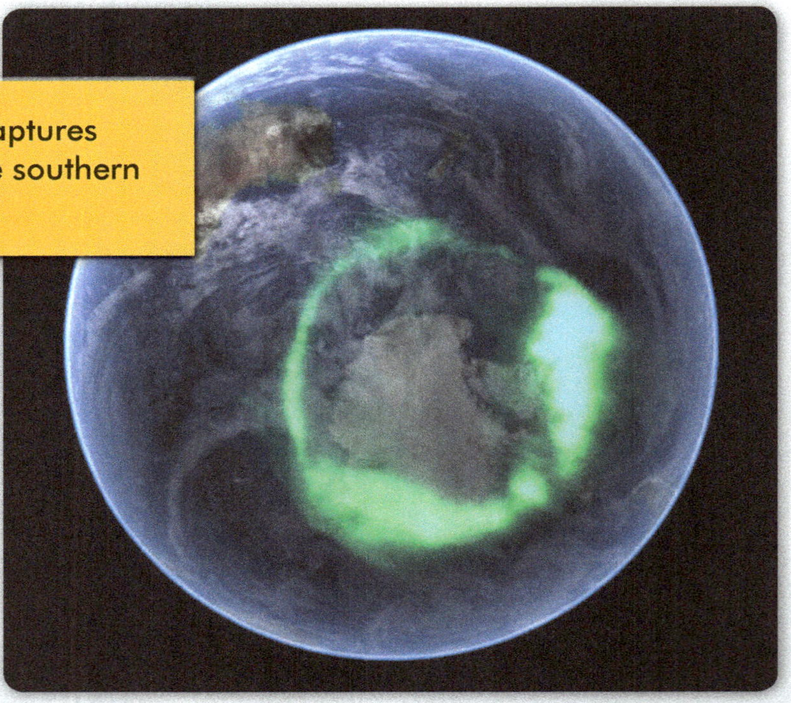

This satellite image captures an auroral oval of the southern lights over Antarctica.

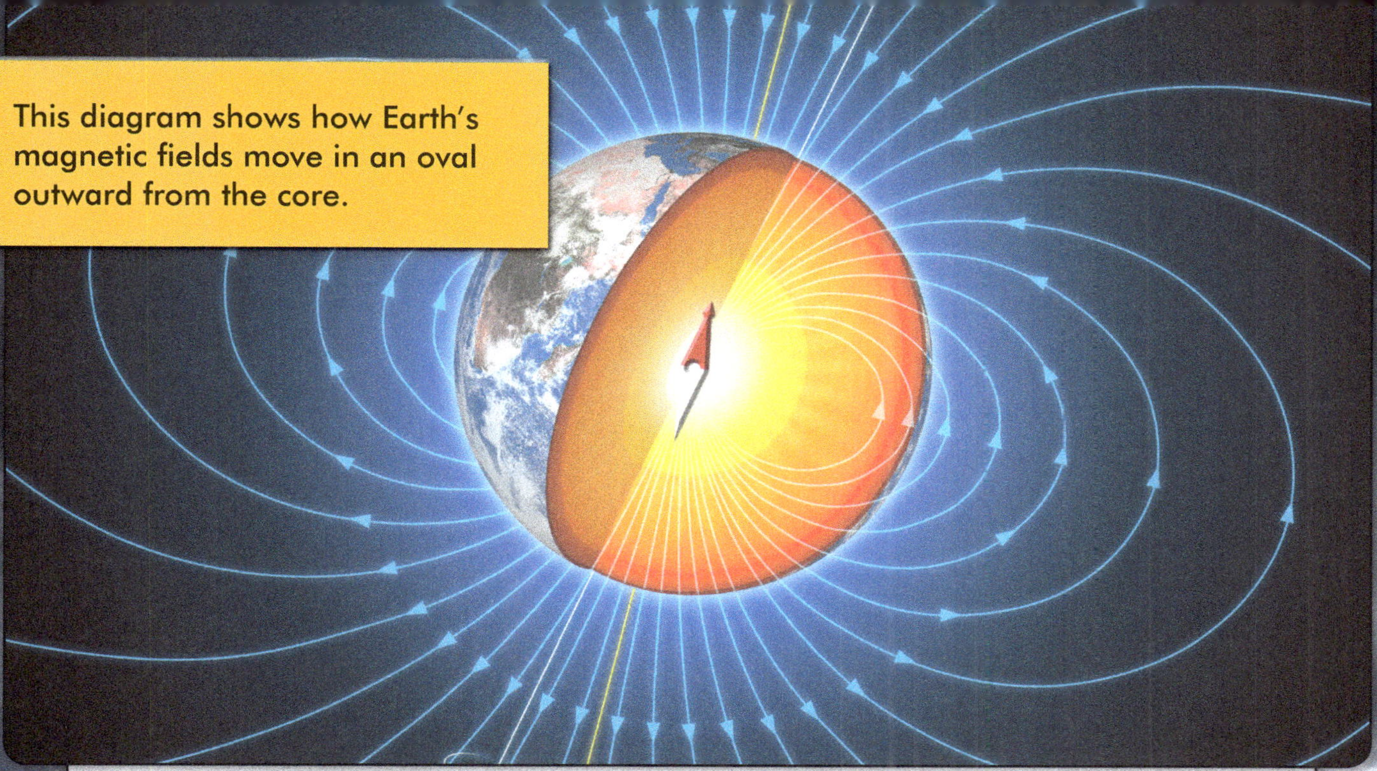

This diagram shows how Earth's magnetic fields move in an oval outward from the core.

They form because Earth behaves as if it has a giant bar magnet inside the planet. The "force-field" lines from Earth's magnetic interior extend out from the tips of the core magnet like a widening cone. When solar particles rain from space they follow the magnetic-field lines down to Earth, trying to converge on the tip of the bar magnet deep inside the planet. The particles hit the atmosphere first, creating twin glowing rings of light. At the bottom of the world, the southern oval creates aurora australis, the southern lights, a mirror image of the more familiar northern lights.

In North America, the northern auroral oval usually shimmers over Alaska and Canada's northern territories, where people see northern lights almost every night. During a powerful solar storm, the auroral oval expands and heads south, bringing glowing lights to the skies of the southern United States and, on rare occasions, even Mexico.

CHAPTER FOUR

AURORAS: TO SEE OR NOT TO SEE

OK, so now that you know what the aurora borealis is all about, the big question is, "Will you ever see it?" Sure! If you're in the right place at the right time. And where that is just might surprise you.

Being farther north certainly helps, but even if you live in a southern state, you still may catch a glimpse of the northern lights on rare occasions. On April 11, 2001, auroras appeared as far south as New Mexico and parts of Texas.

If you live in Barrow, Alaska; Yellowknife in Canada's Northwest Territories; or Tromsø, Norway, you've got it made. Go outside on any clear night, and you're almost guaranteed to see an auroral display. Auroras are always present at high **latitudes** (even during daylight; they're just too faint to see then). They appear in an oval-shaped ring, like a halo around each of the **geomagnetic** poles. These auroral ovals expand and contract depending on the strength and direction of the solar wind, and they are tipped toward Earth's night side, dipping to lower latitudes around midnight. They also bulge toward the equator during geomagnetic storms—the bigger the storm, the closer to the equator.

And that's one of the tricks to seeing the aurora in places like Seattle, Washington, or Topeka, Kansas—a powerful geomagnetic storm. The farther south you are, the higher the geomagnetic activity level needed to push the aurora into your sky. It's not just a matter of pulling out an atlas to check your latitude, though. The problem is that there are two north poles: the geographic north pole (the northern end of Earth's axis), and the magnetic north pole (the "north" to which magnetic compasses point). The two poles are located hundreds of kilometers from each other. The maps in your atlas are based on the geographic north pole and, you guessed it, it's the distance from the magnetic north pole that's important

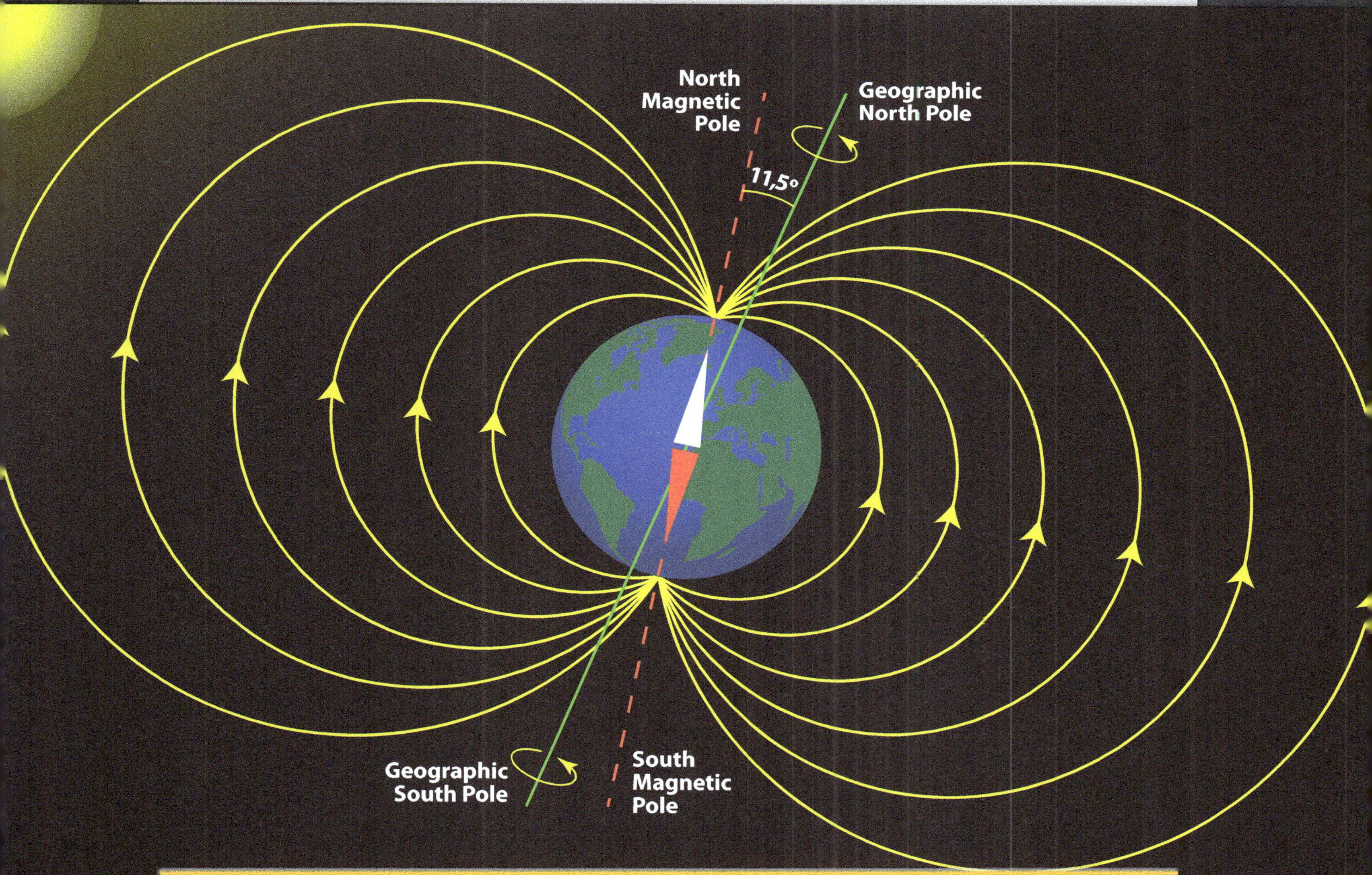

Notice the difference in location between the geographic poles and the magnetic ones. This difference means that your geographic latitude and longitude don't match your geomagnetic longitude and latitude.

These glass igloos in Finland allow tourists to come and see the aurora borealis up close.

when predicting auroras. You need to find your geomagnetic latitude—that's the other trick—which in North America will be about five to ten degrees higher.

Can't wait for a geomagnetic storm to bring the aurora to you? Then you need to take a trip north. Tourist facilities in and near Fairbanks, Alaska, and Yellowknife, Northwest Territories (Canada), are set up to show the aurora to visitors from late spring, through winter, to early spring. To see a nice aurora, plan to stay at least a week and to spend many hours looking at the sky (the three or four hours up to midnight are best). If you fly to your location, arrange to fly in and out at night—you will be above any clouds. Good luck and happy viewing!

GLOSSARY

atomosphere The blanket of gases that surrounds a planet.

atom The most basic unit of matter.

atomic particle The parts of an atom, including protons, neutrons, and electrons.

chemistry The area of science that studies the substances that make up matter and what happens when those substances interact.

corona A blanket of gas that surrounds stars, such as the sun.

electron An atomic particle that has a negative charge.

flare A sudden, intense burst of heat, energy, or light.

gale-force Relating to a very strong wind.

geomagnetic Having to do with Earth's magnetic field.

ionosphere One of the layers that make up Earth's atmosphere.

latitude The north–south location of a point on Earth's surface.

magnetic field The area around a magnet that has magnetic qualities or acts like a magnet.

neon A colorless, odorless gas used in lamps.

nucleus (nuclei) The center of an atom made up of protons and neutrons.

physics The area of science that deals with the nature and properties of matter.

plasma One of the four states of matter that is created by superheating a gas or when a gas is in a strong magnetic field.

proton An atomic particle that has a positive charge.

radiation Energy released in waves or particles.

squall A sudden powerful gust of wind.

time-lapse Describes a filming technique that makes time look like it is moving faster than normal.

ultraviolet A type of radiation given off by the sun.

vacuum A space without matter.

FURTHER READING

BOOKS

Bortolotti, Dan. *Auroras: Fire in the Sky*. Ontario, Canada: Firefly Books, 2011.

Peters, Elisa. *Auroras: Behind the Northern and Southern Lights*. New York, NY: Rosen, 2016.

Rajczak, Kristen. *The Northern Lights*. New York, NY: Gareth Stevens, 2012.

Whitfield, David. *Northern Lights*. New York, NY: Av2 by Weigl, 2012.

WEBSITES

Easy Science for Kids

www.easyscienceforkids.com/all-about-the-northern-lights

Read fun facts about the myths and science surrounding the northern lights.

KidsAstronomy.com

www.kidsastronomy.com/Aurora_article.php

Learn more about the aurora at the northern and southern poles.

Science Kids

www.sciencekids.co.nz/sciencefacts/earth/aurora.html

Discover more interesting information about the northern and southern lights.

INDEX